The Pilot and the Little Prince

THE LIFE OF
ANTOINE DE SAINT-EXUPÉRY

Peter Sís

Frances Foster Books
FARRAR STRAUS GIROUX
New York

The Wind—idea—Bill Shipsey
The Earth—inspiration—Terry Lajtha
The Stars—dreams—Frances Foster

Farrar Straus Giroux Books for Young Readers
175 Fifth Avenue, New York 10010

Copyright © 2014 by Peter Sís
All rights reserved
Color separations by Embassy Graphics Ltd.
Printed in the United States of America by Phoenix Color,
Hagerstown, Maryland
Designed by Andrew Arnold
First edition, 2014
3   5   7   9   10   8   6   4   2

mackids.com

Library of Congress Cataloging-in-Publication Data
Sís, Peter, 1949–
    The Pilot and the Little Prince : the Life of Antoine de Saint-Exupéry / Peter
Sís. — First edition.
        pages cm
    ISBN 978-0-374-38069-4 (hardcover)
    1. Saint-Exupéry, Antoine de, 1900–1944—Juvenile literature.   2. Authors,
French—20th century—Biography.   3. Air pilots—France—Biography.   I. Title.

PQ2637.A274Z8295 2013
848'.91209—dc23
[B]

2013027732

*Thanks to Howard Scherry of Remembering Saint-Exupéry for information on Antoine de Saint-Exupéry's life and
to the Smithsonian National Air and Space Museum and Leo Opdycke for information on early aviation history*

Selected Bibliography

Cate, Curtis. *Antoine de Saint-Exupéry: His Life and Times.* New York: Paragon House, 1990.
Jarrett, Philip. *The Color Encyclopedia of Incredible Airplanes.* New York: Dorling Kindersley,
    2006.
Saint-Exupéry, Antoine de. *The Little Prince.* New York: Harcourt, Inc., 1943.
Saint-Exupéry, Antoine de. *Night Flight.* New York: Harcourt Brace & Company, 1932.
Saint-Exupéry, Antoine de. *Wind, Sand and Stars.* New York: Reynal & Hitchcock, 1940.
Schiff, Stacy. *Saint-Exupéry: A Biography.* New York: Henry Holt and Company, 2006.
    First published in 1994 by Alfred A. Knopf.

Groupe Latécoère Web site: www.latecoere.fr/content/en/About_us/History/

Quote on page 17 from *Antoine de Saint-Exupéry: His Life and Times* by Curtis Cate.
Inscription on page 37 courtesy of Franklin D. Roosevelt Presidential Library.

Farrar Straus Giroux Books for Young Readers may be purchased for business or promotional
use. For information or bulk purchases please contact Macmillan Corporate and Premium Sales
Department at (800) 221-7945 x5422 or by email at specialmarkets@macmillan.com.

Long ago in France, at the turn of the last century, a little boy was born to be an adventurer.

It was an exciting time of discovery in the world. Things people had only dreamed about were being invented—including flying machines.

The boy would grow up to be a pilot. He would write about courageous flights, but also about places you might find if you were to fly long enough and far enough. What did he find on the earth? What did he find in the sky?

Antoine de Saint-Exupéry was born June 29, 1900, in Lyon, France. In his family tree there were an ambassador, a baron, a count, an archbishop, a court chamberlain, knights, scholars, military officers, and musicians.

His father, Count Jean de Saint-Exupéry, died in 1904.

His mother, Countess Marie de Fonscolombe, was a widow at age twenty-eight.

Marie-Madeleine
1897

Simone
1898

François
1902

Gabrielle
1903

Antoine de Saint-Exupéry was born with golden hair. His family called him the Sun King. When he was four years old, his father died unexpectedly. The boy wondered, Where did he go?

Antoine's favorite home was his great-great-aunt's château at Saint-Maurice-de-Rémens, near Lyon.

He also liked to play at his mother's parents' Château de La Môle.

Was his father on a star?

Antoine would wake his family late at night to read them his poetry.

Great-great-aunt

He's so wild!

He's such an angel!

Mother

Antoine spent sunny days playing with his brother and sisters in the loving care of their mother and family. They lived in a big house surrounded by meadows and gardens.

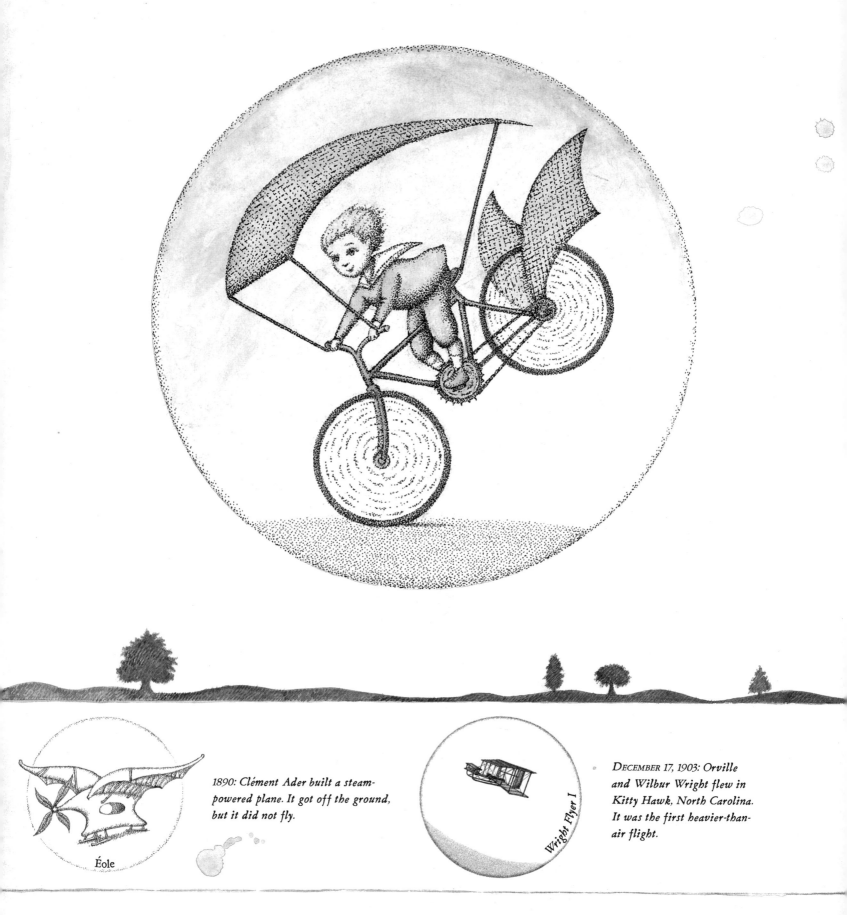

1890: Clément Ader built a steam-powered plane. It got off the ground, but it did not fly.

Éole

DECEMBER 17, 1903: *Orville and Wilbur Wright flew in Kitty Hawk, North Carolina. It was the first heavier-than-air flight.*

Wright Flyer I

Antoine attached sheets to wicker rods on his bicycle to make his plane.

Airplanes had just been invented and France was the center of aviation. When Antoine was twelve years old he made his own flying machine. It did not take off, but this didn't discourage him.

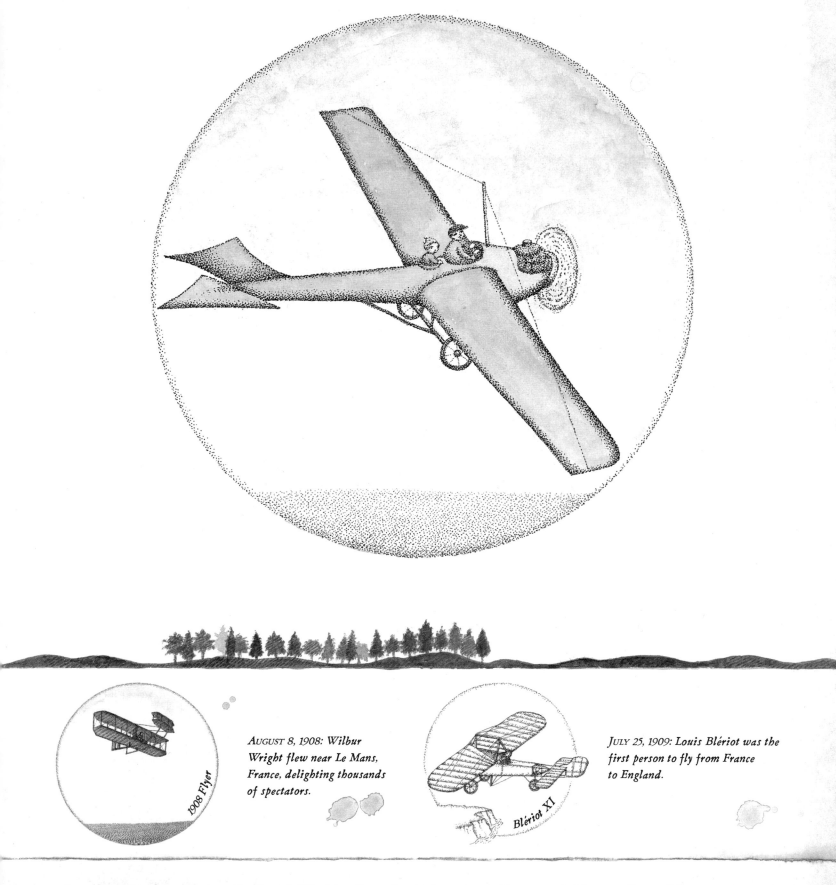

AUGUST 8, 1908: Wilbur Wright flew near Le Mans, France, delighting thousands of spectators.

1908 Flyer

JULY 25, 1909: Louis Blériot was the first person to fly from France to England.

Blériot XI

He got a ride in a Berthaud-Wroblewski at the Ambérieu-en-Bugey airfield, near Saint-Maurice.

That summer, he rode his bike to a nearby airfield every day to watch pilots test planes. He told them he had permission from his mother to fly, so one pilot took him up in the air. His mother was not happy. Antoine couldn't wait to go up again.

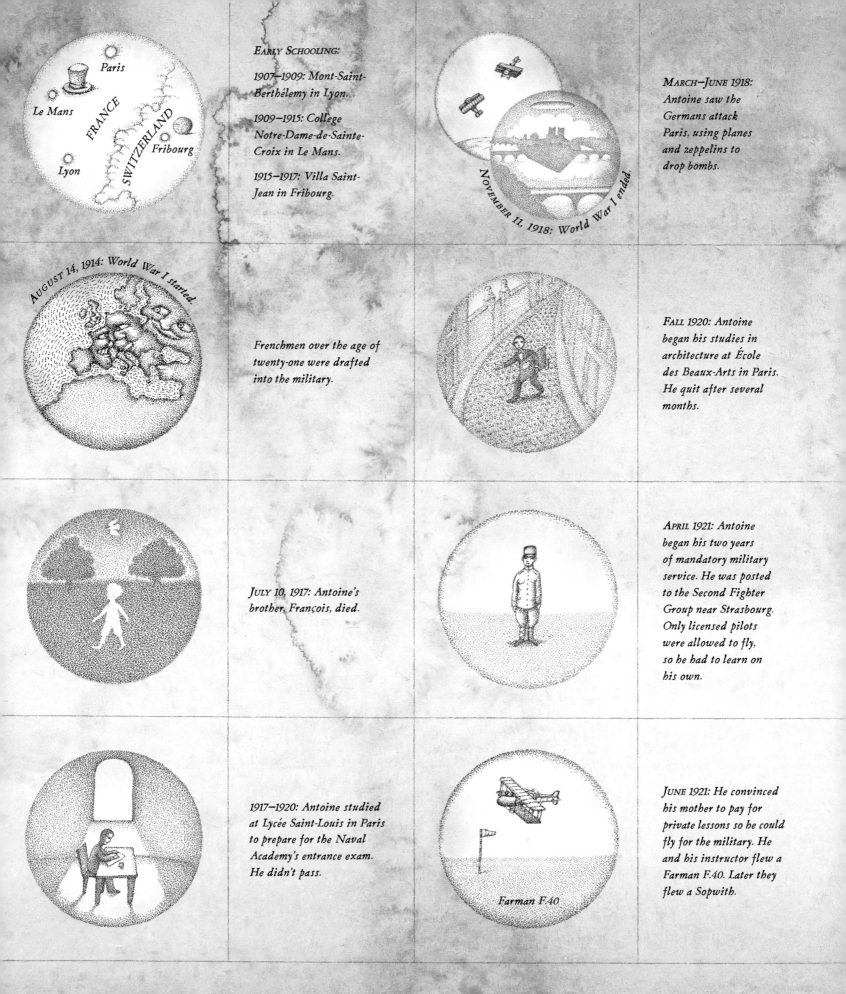

EARLY SCHOOLING:

1907–1909: Mont-Saint-Berthélemy in Lyon.

1909–1915: College Notre-Dame-de-Sainte-Croix in Le Mans.

1915–1917: Villa Saint-Jean in Fribourg.

MARCH–JUNE 1918: *Antoine saw the Germans attack Paris, using planes and zeppelins to drop bombs.*

NOVEMBER 11, 1918: *World War I ended.*

AUGUST 14, 1914: *World War I started.*

Frenchmen over the age of twenty-one were drafted into the military.

FALL 1920: *Antoine began his studies in architecture at École des Beaux-Arts in Paris. He quit after several months.*

JULY 10, 1917: *Antoine's brother, François, died.*

APRIL 1921: *Antoine began his two years of mandatory military service. He was posted to the Second Fighter Group near Strasbourg. Only licensed pilots were allowed to fly, so he had to learn on his own.*

1917–1920: Antoine studied at Lycée Saint-Louis in Paris to prepare for the Naval Academy's entrance exam. He didn't pass.

Farman F.40

JUNE 1921: *He convinced his mother to pay for private lessons so he could fly for the military. He and his instructor flew a Farman F.40. Later they flew a Sopwith.*

Antoine could think only of flying, but his family hoped he would finish his studies and do something less dangerous. When he was called to military duty, he asked for aviation and was assigned to the ground crew. In time, he learned to fly.

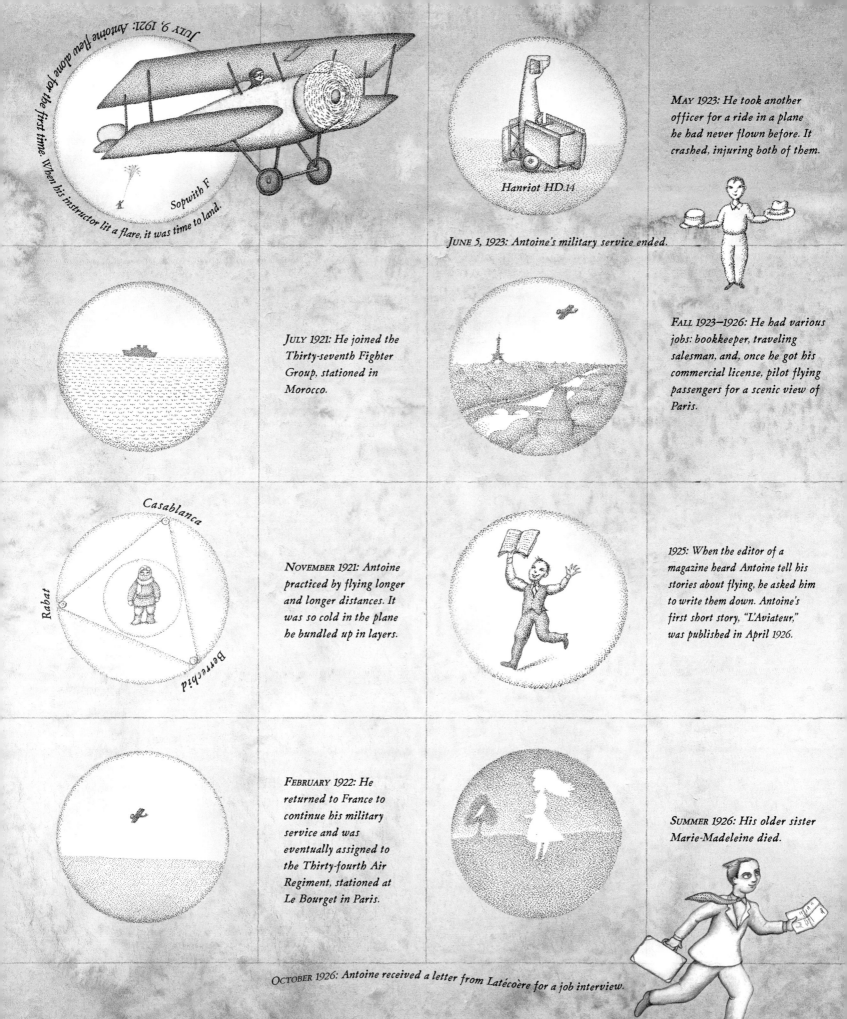

JULY 9, 1921: Antoine flew alone for the first time. When his instructor lit a flare, it was time to land.

Sopwith F

Hanriot HD.14

MAY 1923: He took another officer for a ride in a plane he had never flown before. It crashed, injuring both of them.

JUNE 5, 1923: Antoine's military service ended.

JULY 1921: He joined the Thirty-seventh Fighter Group, stationed in Morocco.

FALL 1923–1926: He had various jobs: bookkeeper, traveling salesman, and, once he got his commercial license, pilot flying passengers for a scenic view of Paris.

Casablanca

Rabat

Berrechid

NOVEMBER 1921: Antoine practiced by flying longer and longer distances. It was so cold in the plane he bundled up in layers.

1925: When the editor of a magazine heard Antoine tell his stories about flying, he asked him to write them down. Antoine's first short story, "L'Aviateur," was published in April 1926.

FEBRUARY 1922: He returned to France to continue his military service and was eventually assigned to the Thirty-fourth Air Regiment, stationed at Le Bourget in Paris.

SUMMER 1926: His older sister Marie-Madeleine died.

OCTOBER 1926: Antoine received a letter from Latécoère for a job interview.

Two years after his service, Antoine heard about an airline that was starting to deliver the mail. This was something that had never been done before and he wanted to be a part of the excitement.

LATÉCOÈRE · AÉROPOSTALE

Pierre-Georges Latécoère created the Latécoère company in 1917 to manufacture airplanes for the French military during World War I. After the war he decided to use the same planes to deliver the mail, and he hired his childhood friend and war veteran Beppo de Massimi to help him. Letters that used to take weeks to arrive could now be delivered in days. There were other start-up mail airlines, but Latécoère had the most extensive routes, flying first from Toulouse, France, to other cities in France and Spain, then expanding to the French colonies in West Africa and on to South America. In 1927 Latécoère sold its airline division to Aéropostale but continued to manufacture planes.

Pierre-Georges Latécoère
Company Founder

Several of the pilots Latécoère hired were World War I flying aces—men Antoine had admired as a teenager. Some of them became his friends, and later he made them heroes in his books.

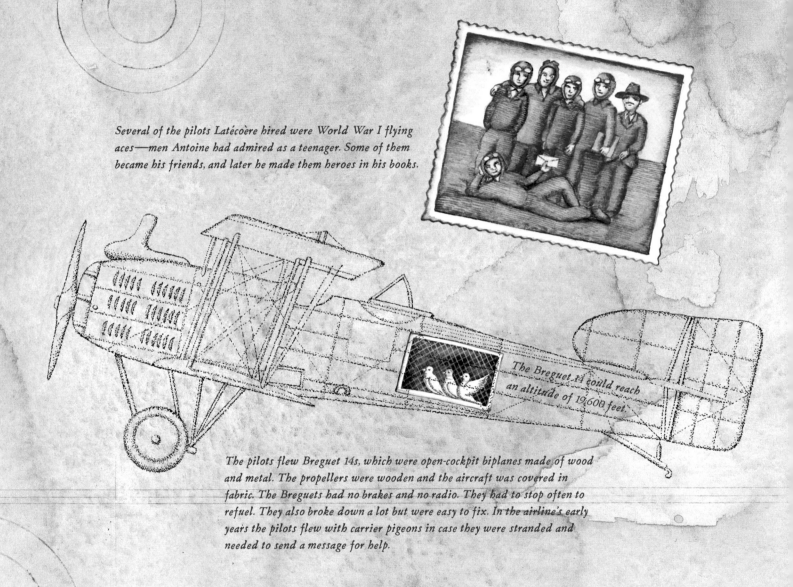

The Breguet 14 could reach
an altitude of 19,600 feet.

The pilots flew Breguet 14s, which were open-cockpit biplanes made of wood and metal. The propellers were wooden and the aircraft was covered in fabric. The Breguets had no brakes and no radio. They had to stop often to refuel. They also broke down a lot but were easy to fix. In the airline's early years the pilots flew with carrier pigeons in case they were stranded and needed to send a message for help.

Antoine de Saint-Exupéry
Pilot

The airline hired him! Like everybody new to the company, Antoine started as a mechanic. Soon he tested planes, took short trips for practice, and learned by flying with other pilots who were delivering the mail.

Elysée Negrin
Pilot

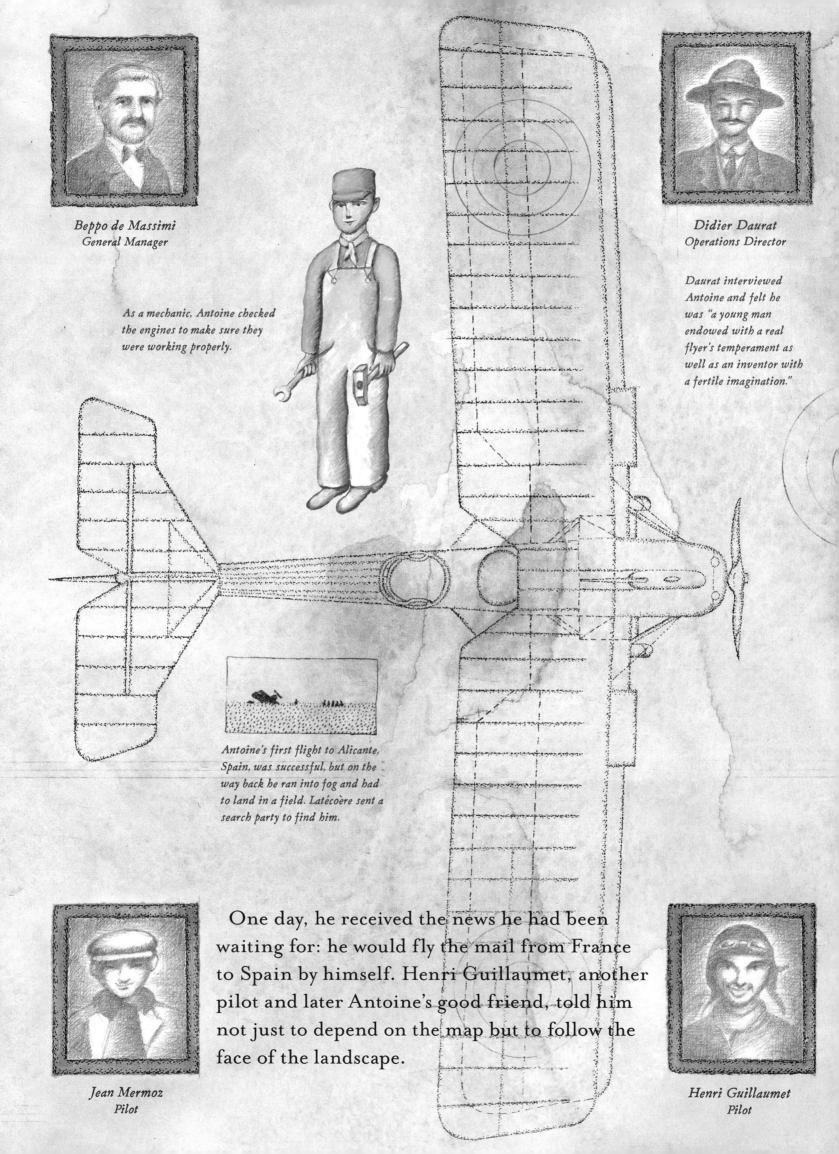

Beppo de Massimi
General Manager

As a mechanic, Antoine checked the engines to make sure they were working properly.

Didier Daurat
Operations Director

Daurat interviewed Antoine and felt he was "a young man endowed with a real flyer's temperament as well as an inventor with a fertile imagination."

Antoine's first flight to Alicante, Spain, was successful, but on the way back he ran into fog and had to land in a field. Latécoère sent a search party to find him.

One day, he received the news he had been waiting for: he would fly the mail from France to Spain by himself. Henri Guillaumet, another pilot and later Antoine's good friend, told him not just to depend on the map but to follow the face of the landscape.

Jean Mermoz
Pilot

Henri Guillaumet
Pilot

FRANCE

Toulouse

Perpignan

SPAIN

Barcelona

Gibraltar

Alicante

Málaga

Ceuta

Tangier

Rabat

MOROCCO

Casablanca

Cape Juby

WESTERN SAHARA

Villa Cisneros

Port-Étienne

Dakar

SENEGAL

FEBRUARY 1927. The plane taking Antoine to his post in Dakar crashed and he was left alone to guard it.

From Dakar, the mail was shipped to South America.

Antoine was six feet two inches tall and had a hard time fitting in the cockpit.

At this time, France, Spain, Great Britain, Germany, Belgium, Italy, and Portugal all had colonies in Africa.

The pilots went up rain or shine.

They flew below the clouds so they could see.

The planes were noisy, so pilot and passenger had to pass notes.

MAY 21, 1927: Charles Lindbergh flew from New York City to Paris.

Spirit of St. Louis

Being a pioneer air mail pilot was everything Antoine dreamed it would be. He flew in Europe and then along the West African coast, where sometimes two planes traveled together in case one broke down or crashed. When the stars began to light up the sky, he knew it was time to land.

Antoine's house was next to a Spanish fort that held prisoners.

He had a water jug, a basin, a gramophone and books.

Once a month a boat from the Canary Islands delivered supplies.

The planes needed to refuel often, so the airline had an arrangement with the Spanish government to land in their territory.

The airline put Antoine in charge of an airfield in Cape Juby. He lived in a wooden shack and had few belongings and fewer visitors. With an ocean on one side and desert everywhere else, it seemed like one of the loneliest places in the world. But he loved the solitude and being under millions of stars.

Guillaumet crashed in a swamp, and Antoine and another pilot had to help him get out.

Antoine tamed animals for company.

Acting as an ambassador for the airline, Antoine entertained officers from the fort and local nomads.

Some nomads flew in the planes as translators. The pilots thought they were better guides than their compasses.

Antoine rescued stranded flyers. He negotiated with hostile nomads who had shot down planes and held pilots for ransom. He made peace with others, who called him Captain of the Birds. His life in the desert inspired him to write.

The pilots who created the South American lines were the Frenchmen Jean Mermoz, Henri Guillaumet, Marcel Reine, Paul Vachet, and Antoine de Saint-Exupéry and the Argentinean Vicente Almandos Almonacid.

Saint-Louis, Senegal

Port of Natal, Brazil

MAY 12–13, 1930: Jean Mermoz and crew flew across the Atlantic Ocean in a Latécoère 28 fitted with floats.

SOUTHERN MAIL

Published July 1929

When planes flew across the ocean at night, the pilots navigated by the stars, compasses, and ships lit with beacons.

The governments of Argentina, Uruguay, Chile, Paraguay, Peru, and Bolivia agreed to let the pilots fly in their countries.

Eager to explore other skies, Antoine joined his fellow aviators in creating new mail routes in South America. Nothing could stop them as they crossed glaciers, rain forests, and mountain peaks, battling fierce winds and wild storms.

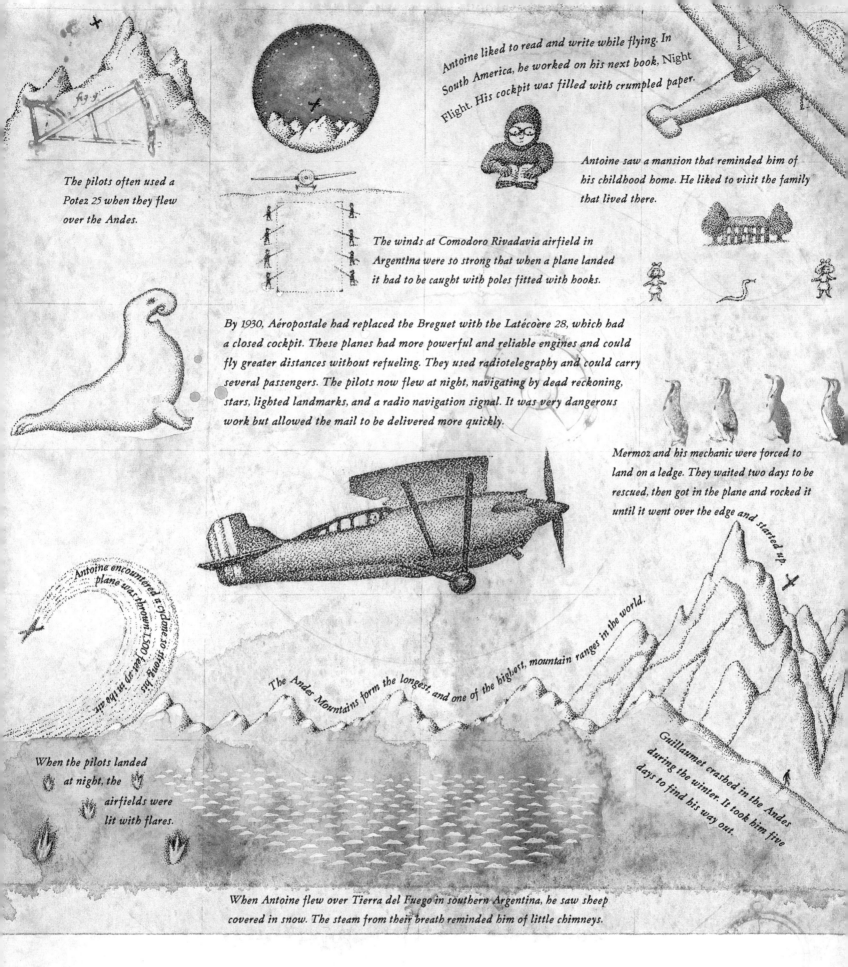

The pilots often used a Potez 25 when they flew over the Andes.

Antoine liked to read and write while flying. In South America, he worked on his next book, Night Flight. His cockpit was filled with crumpled paper.

Antoine saw a mansion that reminded him of his childhood home. He liked to visit the family that lived there.

The winds at Comodoro Rivadavia airfield in Argentina were so strong that when a plane landed it had to be caught with poles fitted with hooks.

By 1930, Aéropostale had replaced the Breguet with the Latécoère 28, which had a closed cockpit. These planes had more powerful and reliable engines and could fly greater distances without refueling. They used radiotelegraphy and could carry several passengers. The pilots now flew at night, navigating by dead reckoning, stars, lighted landmarks, and a radio navigation signal. It was very dangerous work but allowed the mail to be delivered more quickly.

Mermoz and his mechanic were forced to land on a ledge. They waited two days to be rescued, then got in the plane and rocked it until it went over the edge and started up.

Antoine encountered a cyclone so strong his plane was thrown 1,500 feet up in the air.

The Andes Mountains form the longest, and one of the highest, mountain ranges in the world.

When the pilots landed at night, the airfields were lit with flares.

Guillaumet crashed in the Andes during the winter. It took him five days to find his way out.

When Antoine flew over Tierra del Fuego in southern Argentina, he saw sheep covered in snow. The steam from their breath reminded him of little chimneys.

Antoine was Flight Director of Aéropostale's Argentina operation and helped open the Buenos Aires–to–Río Gallegos route.

Antoine spent more time in the air here than anywhere else because the pilots now also flew at night. With stars above and lights below, his world felt both immense and small.

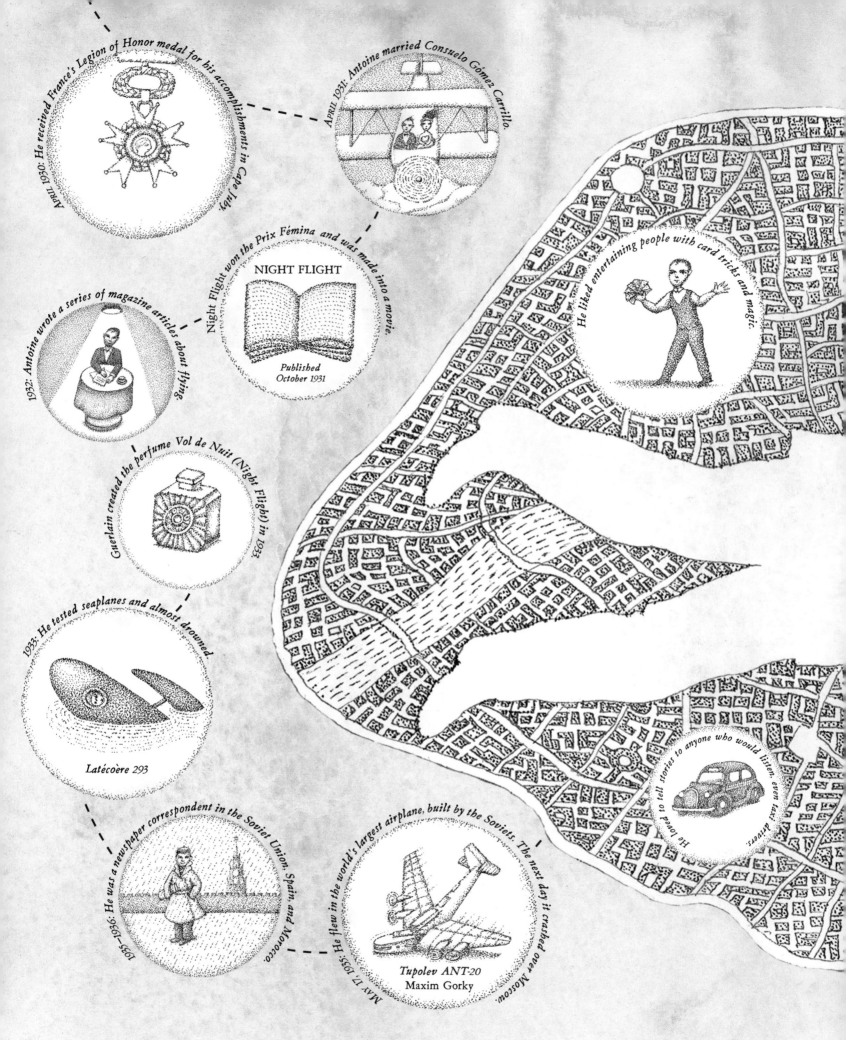

APRIL 1930: He received France's Legion of Honor medal for his accomplishments in Cape Juby.

APRIL 1931: Antoine married Consuelo Gómez Carrillo.

1932: Antoine wrote a series of magazine articles about flying.

Night Flight won the Prix Fémina and was made into a movie.

NIGHT FLIGHT

Published
October 1931

Guerlain created the perfume Vol de Nuit (Night Flight) in 1933

1933: He tested seaplanes and almost drowned.

Latécoère 293

1935–1936: He was a newspaper correspondent in the Soviet Union, Spain, and Morocco.

May 17, 1935: He flew in the world's largest airplane, built by the Soviets. The next day it crashed over Moscow.

Tupolev ANT-20
Maxim Gorky

He liked entertaining people with card tricks and magic.

He loved to tell stories to anyone who would listen, even taxi drivers.

Eventually, Antoine returned to France. He got married. The airline he helped build went out of business, so he looked for new opportunities in life.

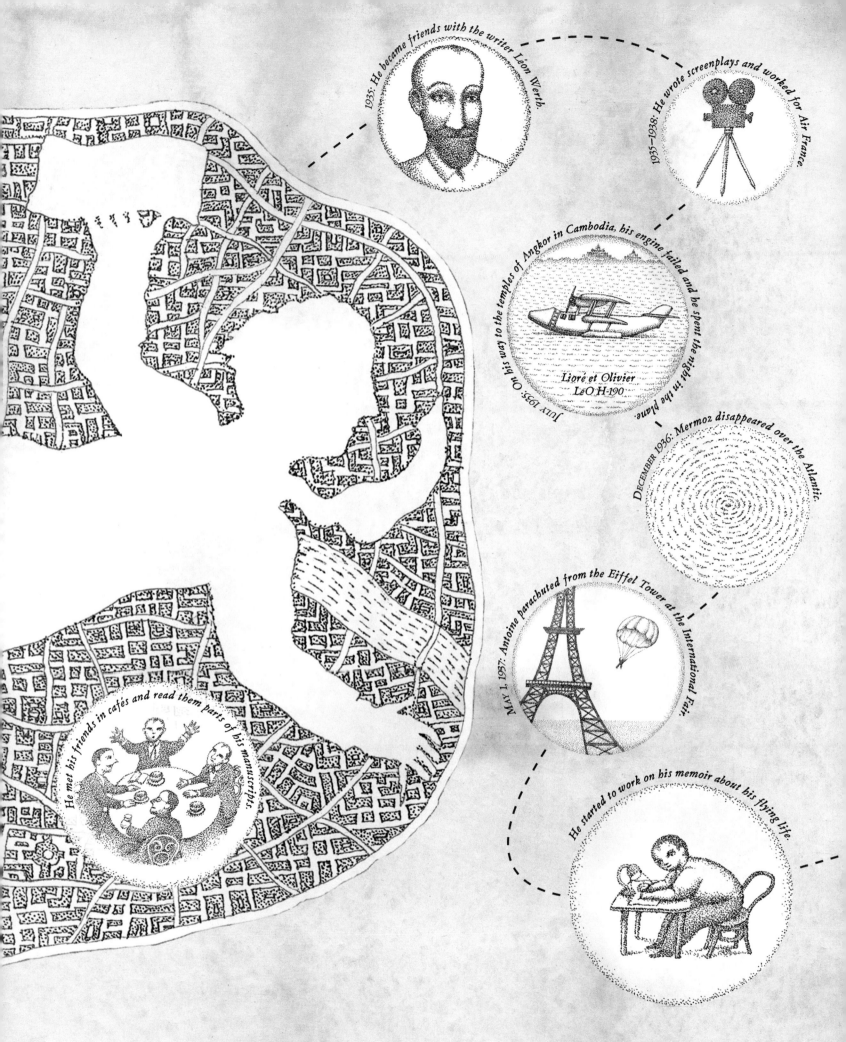

1935: He became friends with the writer Léon Werth.

1935–1938: He wrote screenplays and worked for Air France.

July 1935: On his way to the temples of Angkor in Cambodia, his engine failed and he spent the night in the plane.

Lioré et Olivier
LeO H-190

December 1936: Mermoz disappeared over the Atlantic.

May 1, 1937: Antoine parachuted from the Eiffel Tower at the International Fair.

He started to work on his memoir about his flying life.

He met his friends in cafés and read them parts of his manuscripts.

He had become a well-known pilot and a celebrated writer. Through it all he continued to fly—for work, pleasure, and adventure.

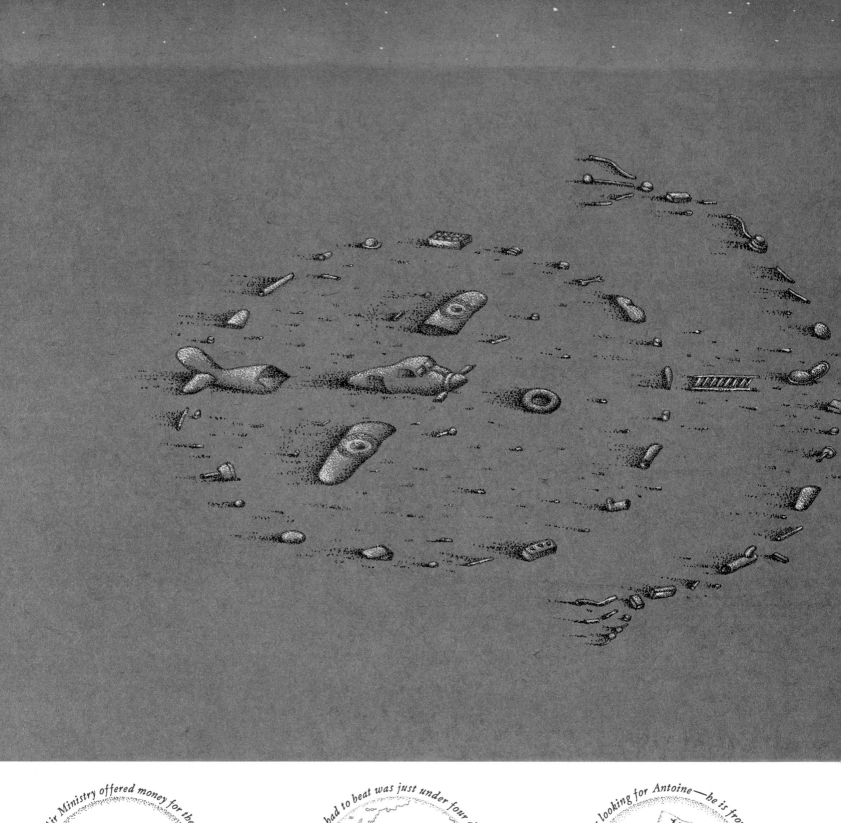

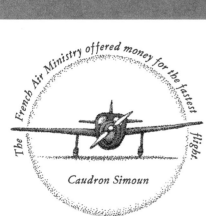

The French Air Ministry offered money for the fastest flight.

Caudron Simoun

The record Antoine had to beat was just under four days and three hours.

Paris

Saigon

The world is looking for Antoine—he is front-page news!

Antoine and his mechanic, André Prévot, left from Paris on December 29, 1935, at 7:01 a.m.

His most famous adventure came when he tried to win a prize for the fastest flight from Paris to Saigon. He and his mechanic were ahead of the existing record when suddenly, in the middle of the night, they were engulfed in layers of clouds.

He and his mechanic wrote a giant message in the sand.

They had only a few leftovers from their plane to survive on.

Bedouins led them to safety.

The plane went down in the Libyan Desert on December 30, 1935, at 2:46 a.m.

Antoine thought he saw a beacon of light. He tried to reach it, got lost, and crashed in North Africa. The plane was destroyed but the two men were not hurt. They wandered in the desert for days before being rescued.

Their plane was crated and they sailed across the ocean on the Île de France

Caudron Simoun

Antoine thought he was in worse condition than the plane.

Antoine and André Prévot left New York on February 15, 1938, and landed in Guatemala on the 16th.

Antoine kept on dreaming up new expeditions. He tried to be the first French pilot to fly from New York to the tip of South America. After several stops, the plane made it as far as Guatemala City to refuel, but it crashed on takeoff. Pulled from the rubble, Antoine was grateful to have survived.

WIND, SAND AND STARS

Winner of the French Academy's Grand Prix du Roman and of America's National Book Award.

Published March 1939

Antoine's first mission was in March 1940. He used an oxygen mask for the first time and wore a pressurized suit to stay warm.

Bloch 174

The Germans had more, and better, planes than the French.

On November 26, 1939, Antoine was assigned to the 2/33 Reconnaissance Group in Orconte, France.

He returned to Paris to heal and to write. But the world around him was veering toward conflict. In September 1939, France declared war on Germany, and Antoine was called up for military duty. He trained with an aviation unit to photograph the location of the enemy. He was now a war pilot.

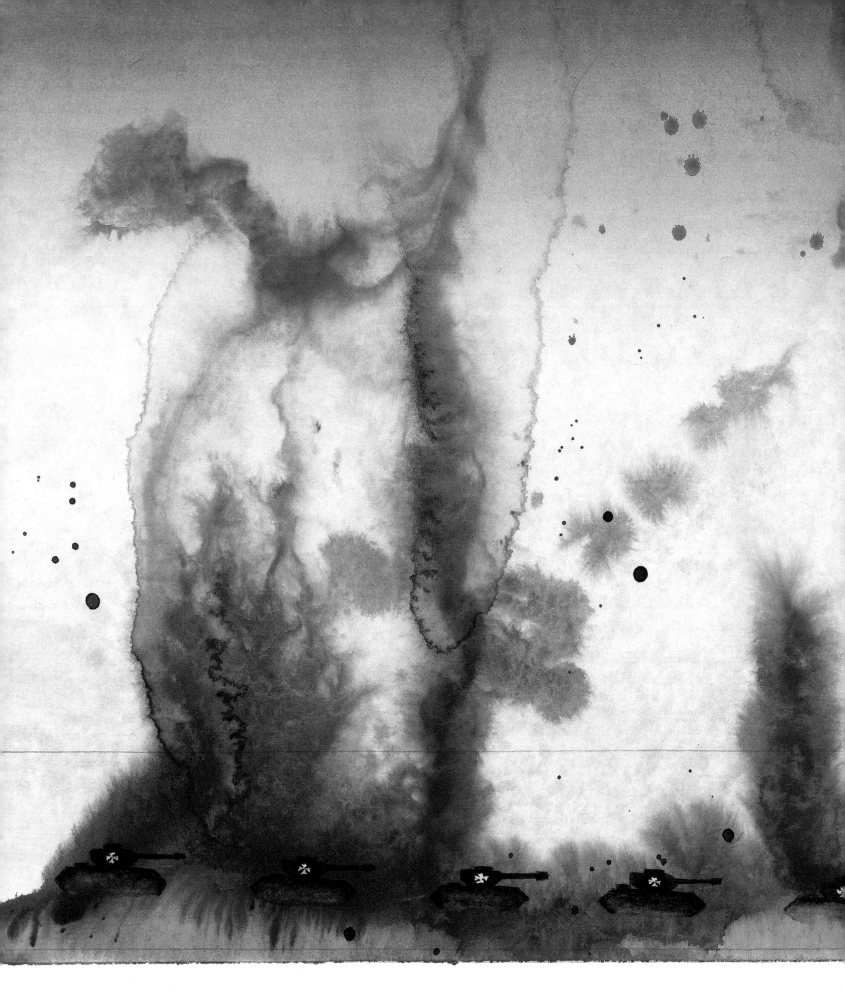

From the skies, Antoine watched the fires, smoke, and destruction the Germans left in their wake as they swooped down from the north. They invaded France on May 10, 1940, and the country fell in just thirty-eight days. Antoine's unit was ordered to North Africa and his service was over.

Back in France, he realized he could not live under German occupation. He fled to Lisbon to board a ship for New York and learned that his friend Guillaumet had been shot down. As Antoine sailed across the ocean under the night sky, he knew he had lost his friend and his country.

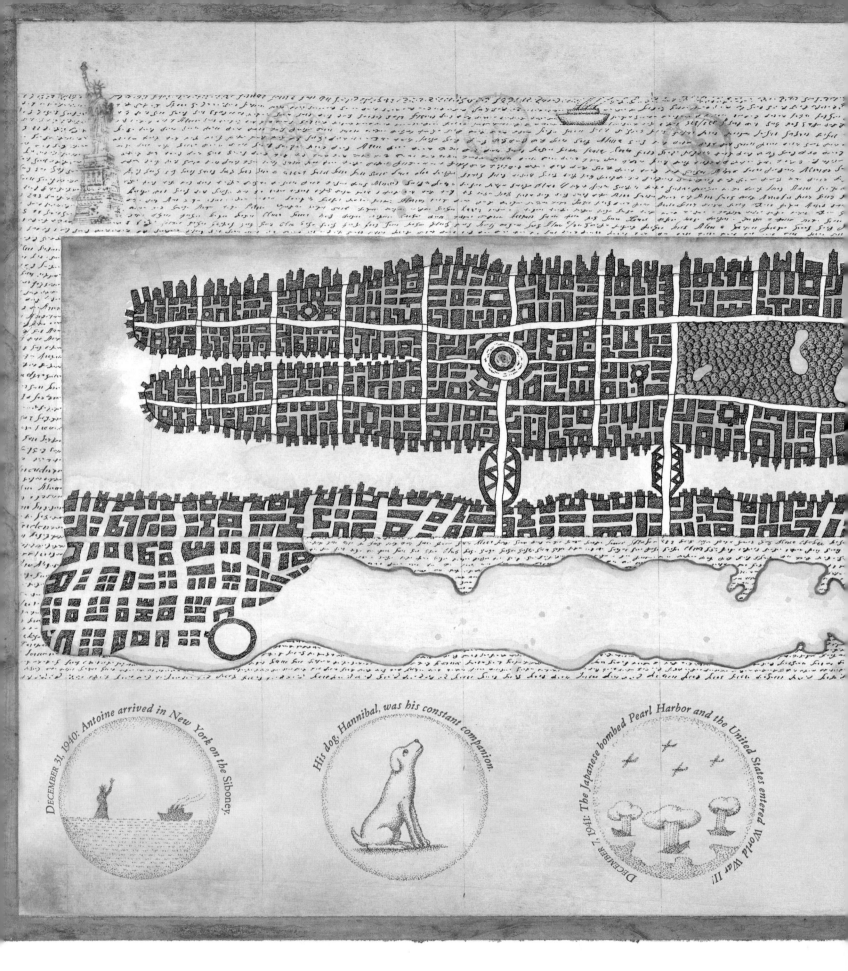

He spent his first year in the United States writing Flight to Arras.

Antoine found New York overwhelming. He didn't speak English and felt out of place, no longer flying but endlessly contemplating the direction the world was taking.

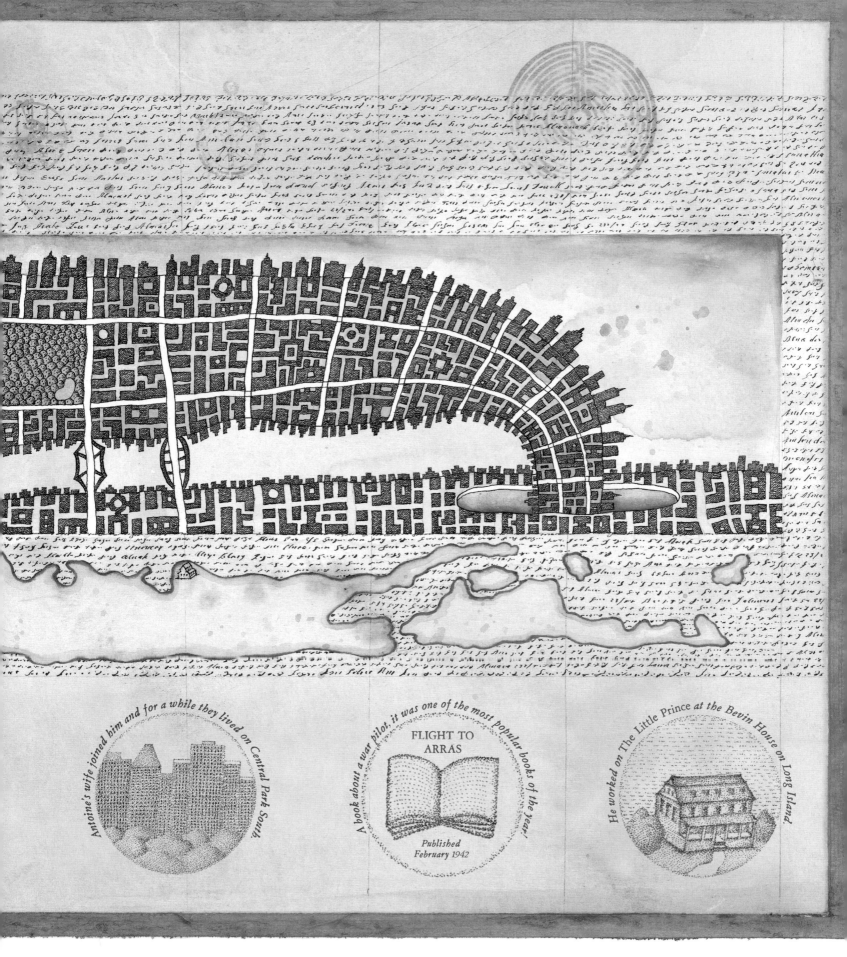

Antoine's wife joined him and for a while they lived on Central Park South.

FLIGHT TO ARRAS

A book about a war pilot, it was one of the most popular books of the year!

Published February 1942

He worked on The Little Prince at the Bevin House on Long Island.

He sent an inscribed copy to President Roosevelt expressing his thanks: "For President Franklin Roosevelt, whose country is taking on the heavy burden of saving the world."

He thought back to his childhood, the places he had seen, the things he had done, and the people he had met. He bought a small box of watercolor paints and started working on an illustrated book about a boy with golden hair.

Antoine made a speech on the radio expressing his patriotism.

"An Open Letter to Frenchmen Everywhere"

He was also an inventor. He tested his ideas about wave power in the bathtub.

He loved to play with children and sometimes made them paper airplanes.

In April 1943, *The Little Prince* was published. In it he described a planet more innocent than his own, with a boy who ventured far from home, questioned how things worked, and searched for answers.

He reenlisted in the French Air Force in early 1943.

He had a special uniform made by the Brooks Uniform Company.

THE LITTLE PRINCE

The Little Prince was first published in the United States. It was dedicated to his friend Léon Werth.

Published April 6, 1943

He set sail on the Stirling Castle, *part of an American troop convoy, on April 13, 1943.*

Antoine had been in New York for over two years and he missed France. He wanted to fly again.

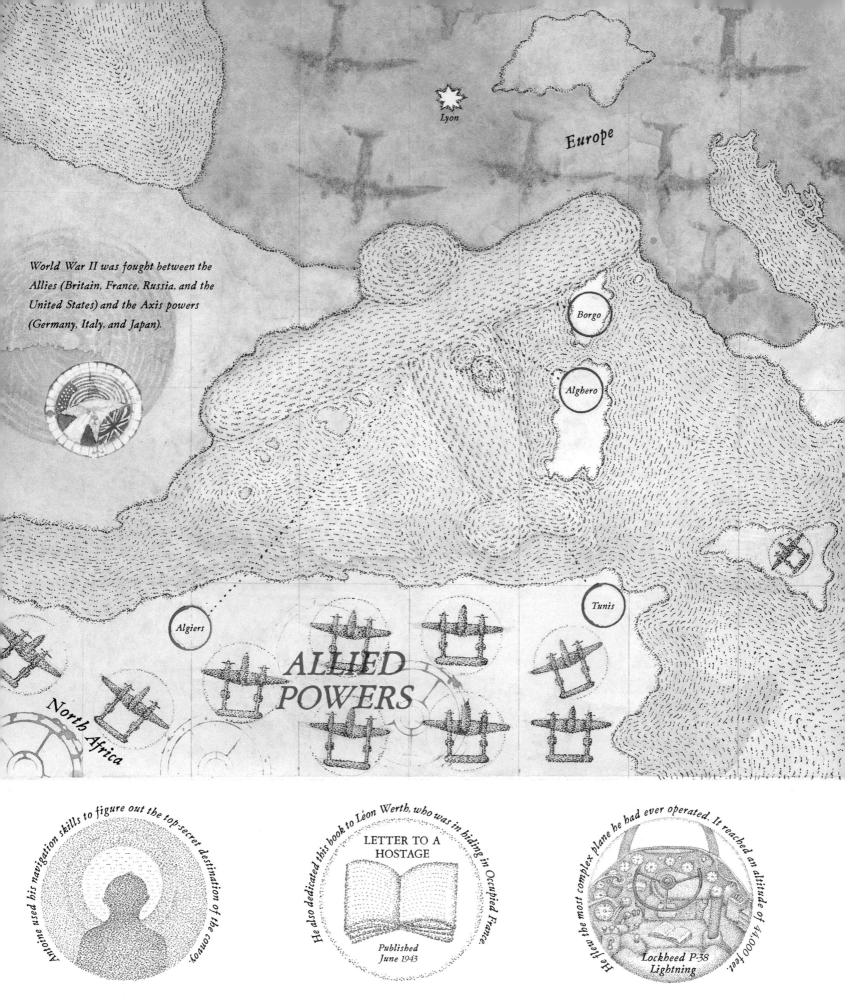

World War II was fought between the Allies (Britain, France, Russia, and the United States) and the Axis powers (Germany, Italy, and Japan).

Lyon

Europe

Borgo

Alghero

Tunis

Algiers

ALLIED POWERS

North Africa

Antoine used his navigation skills to figure out the top-secret destination of the convoy.

He also dedicated this book to Léon Werth, who was in hiding in Occupied France.

LETTER TO A HOSTAGE

Published June 1943

He flew the most complex plane he had ever operated. It reached an altitude of 44,000 feet.

Lockheed P-38 Lightning

The 2/33 Reconnaissance Group was now part of the Allied forces.

Antoine joined his old squadron in North Africa. He asked for flights that would send him over southern France, where his family was living.

AXIS POWERS

The 2/33 Reconnaissance Group was part of the Mediterranean Allied Photo Reconnaissance Wing (MAPRW), made up of British, American, and French pilots. Antoine flew with them from June to August 1943, when he was grounded for crashing a plane on the runway, and then rejoined them in May 1944.

Mediterranean Sea

ANTOINE DE SAINT-EXUPÉRY'S

COMPLETED MISSIONS:

7/21/43: From Tunis over southern France

6/14/44: From Alghero over the Rodez region

6/23/44: From Alghero over southern France

6/29/44: From Alghero over southern France

7/11/44: From Alghero over the Alps

7/14/44: From Alghero over Annecy region

7/18/44: From Borgo over the Alps

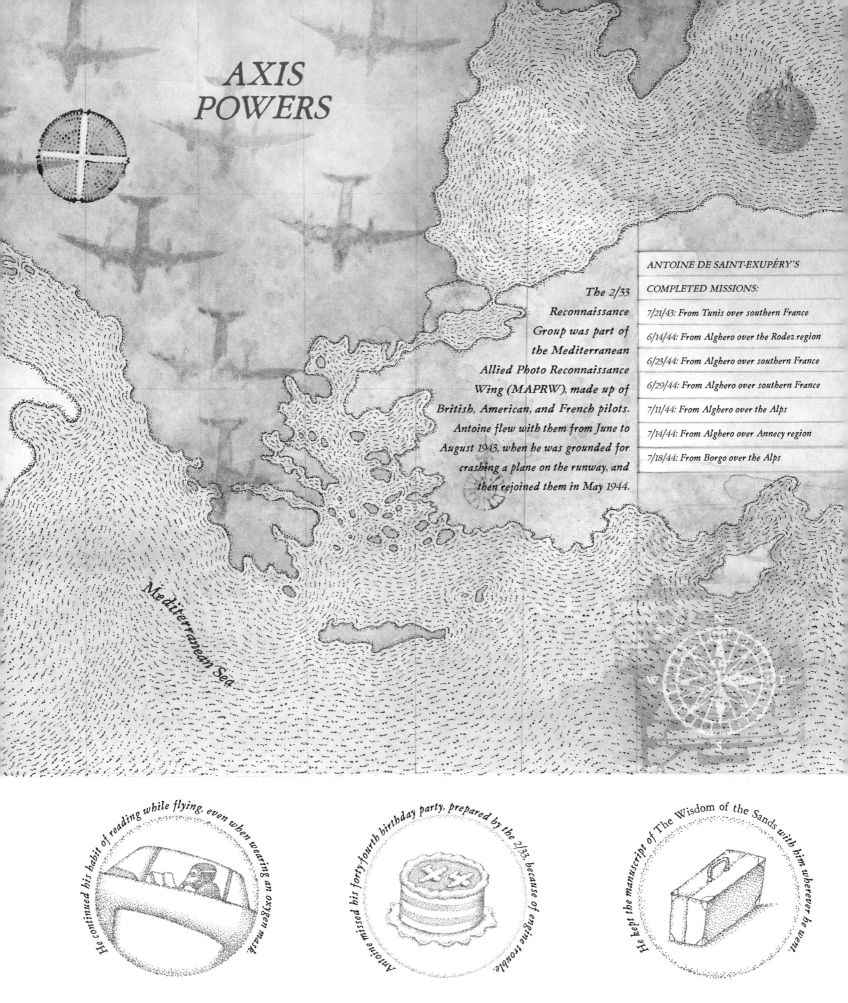

He continued his habit of reading while flying, even when wearing an oxygen mask.

Antoine missed his forty-fourth birthday party, prepared by the 2/33, because of engine trouble.

He kept the manuscript of The Wisdom of the Sands with him wherever he went.

They first flew from Algiers. Then, as more cities were liberated, they moved closer to France.

On July 31, 1944, at 8:45 a.m., he took off from Borgo, Corsica, to photograph enemy positions east of Lyon. It was a beautiful day. He was due back at 12:30.

But he never returned. Some say he forgot his oxygen mask and vanished at sea.

Maybe Antoine found his own glittering planet next to the stars.